Be the Change You Wish to See

Poems and Prose to Inspire and Excite in this Ever-Changing World We Get to Share

Edited by Sueann Wells

Photography by Jennifer DeVille Catalano

Spirited Muse Press
spiritedmusepress.com

ISBN: 978-1-387-84632-0
Copyright 2018 Spirited Muse Press

All rights reserved. No part of this publication may be reproduced, distributed, or transmitted in any form or by any means, including photocopying, recording, or other electronic or mechanical methods, without the prior permission of the author or publisher, except in the case of brief quotations embodied in reviews and certain other noncommercial uses permitted by copyright law.

Cover photo, *The Essence of Love*, and all internal photographs remain the property of Jennifer DeVille Catalano, unless otherwise noted, and may not be reproduced in any form without each photographer's consent.

For reprint permission, to arrange readings, and to order additional copies, contact the editor directly at SpiritedMusePress@yahoo.com. Visit the press online at spiritedmusepress.com

Table of Contents

Editor's Note   7

Chapter I: Be the Best *You* You Can Be   9

A Heart Unlocked   10
   Ginny Riedman-Dangler
Marvel   11
   Jennifer DeVille Catalano
Fearless   12
   Jennifer DeVille Catalano
Solitary   13
   Rachael Z. Ikins
Black Bear   15
   Angie Toh
What is a Woman?   16
   Sue Vogt
Interloper   19
   Sueann Wells
Dancing with Shadows   22
   Jennifer DeVille Catalano
Shadow Dancer   23
   Jennifer DeVille Catalano
In Search of Peace   23
   Sueann Wells
Creek Peace at Low Tide   25
   Sueann Wells
One's Uniqueness   26
   Ginny Riedman-Dangler

Love Grows on Trees   27
    Jennifer DeVille Catalano
We Look into Each Other's Eyes   28
    Rachael Z. Ikins
Infinite Charm   30
    Jennifer DeVille Catalano
In the Woods   30
    Sueann Wells
Après Charles E. Burchfield   33
    Karla Linn Merrifield

Chapter II: Make a Change in Your World   **34**

Poets of the Resistance Resist   35
    Karla Linn Merrifield
Losing Weight   36
    Rachael Z. Ikins
Leave-taking   38
    Rachael Z. Ikins
Lost Babies   40
    Rachael Z. Ikins
Innocence   42
    Sueann Wells
The Power of Parents   43
    Laila Suleiman Dahan
Beginning Again   45
    Jennifer DeVille Catalano
Sweet Tea   47
    Jennifer DeVille Catalano

Dear Parents: Your Children Watch and Learn	48
Laila Suleiman Dahan	
New Day	51
Karla Linn Merrifield	
Catch More Flies with Honey	52
Sue Vogt	
Write with Light	54
Jennifer DeVille Catalano	
Hugs are Better than Slugs	55
Sue Vogt	
Selbstgefälligkeit erzeugt eine Katastrophe	57
Sueann Wells	
Complacency Breeds Disaster	59
Sueann Wells	
What Peace Is	60
Kayla Wells	
Afternoon Light	61
Jennifer DeVille Catalano	
Build Bridges Not Walls	62
Sue Vogt	
Discussion Group Questions	**63**
About the Contributors	**65**

Editor's Note

As an active participant on this earth we get to share, I implore readers to consider your own identity. Who are you in this life? Are you a role model, or could you live and do better? I don't mean first world socioeconomic terms; I mean simple human being, productive, representative members of this species, terms.

What are you doing to make the world a better place? It seems so cliché, but hey, isn't it insane that we still have to think about it? How sad for humanity. I often hike and take off my egocentric human glasses for a wider worldview, and I find myself sad at the state of human affairs today.

Why must people fight? Why must people volley for attention as though they are any better than the next person? Why can't people just 'get along'? We can do better.

Let's each do our part to be the best human beings we can be, and spread the goodness of humanity. Do what's Right, even when it's hard, even when the easy choice presents itself and you're tempted. Be the best *You* you can be, and let your self shine as inspiration to the next person. It will snowball, and humanity will be better for it.

Take a read through these women's pieces. Consider their value. Consider how the authors grapple with challenges and rise to be better people in their lives. Know you can do the same in yours, in even the most seemingly-insignificant piece of your realm. You *can* make a difference.

We can. We will. We must make the world a better place.

Thank you, contributors, for sharing your works, your voices. Readers, thank you for sharing them now. Please savor them, and share them widely. In this way, our voices will shine above the darkness, and we can make a difference in the gloom. By writing our hearts, we will make the change we wish to see.

Please consider contributing your own voices next time you have the opportunity. Seek venues to shine your light. You are valid in your experiences and your voices. Let's all listen to each other and speak our hearts.

In peace,

Sueann

I

Be The Best *You* You Can Be

A Heart Unlocked

Hanging high, so frozen and clear;
We can only observe them
when winter is here.

Frozen and frigid
throughout the season they stay-
However, when the rays of the sun kiss them,
they begin to melt away.

Warmth and acceptance
they receive from the sun,
giving them strength to risk--
so in time, icicles, there are none.

Glistening rays then shine through
as the icicles melt.
In time, only life-giving
Spring will be felt.

Never underestimate the rays
that radiate through you.
For when you least expect it
a heart may melt and be unlocked
because of you.

Ginny Riedman-Dangler

Marvel

At her age, I was afraid to touch the pages of books with "scary" pictures on them. I flipped past the lifelike diagrams of frog anatomy in the *World Book Encyclopedia* as quickly as possible, terrified of the exposed organs. I worried that the photographs of sharks, squid, and jellyfish featured in each month's issue of *National Geographic* might somehow jump off the page to bite me or sting me.

She stares at nature magazines, absorbing every last detail. She hijacks my iPhone to ask Siri questions about coyotes, stingrays, and tarantulas. Her fingers swipe the touchscreen with ease and confidence as she zooms in on photographs of wildlife.

Spiders still scare me, but she doesn't mind them at all. I've been known to jump when a snake slithers across my path, or gasp when I find one sunning itself atop the lavender bushes. I try not to overreact, though, because I don't want to teach her trepidation of the natural world. I was schooled in fear, but she need not be. She came into this world both adventurous and brave. The only tears shed on her first day of nursery school were mine. I admire how comfortable she is in new environments, and how quickly she absorbs information.

I want to encourage her sense of discovery rather than squelch it. And so, even when she brings me a newly molted snakeskin that she found in the garden, I don't flinch. Instead, I marvel at her fearlessness.

Jennifer DeVille Catalano

Fearless
Jennifer DeVille Catalano

Solitary

She paces a path, ignores screaming
children who smear fingers on
the glass that protects her from them
two inches away.
Her shaggy head swings
side to side, black fur uneven.
You wonder if she has a skin condition.

You read on a sign next to her planted prison that
she is the only species of bear
to carry babies on her back
with thick fur cubs can grip.

Kids stand on rocks next to the other sign,
"Don't stand on the rocks!"
They climb over wire meant to keep them out.
Parents jabber into cell phones.

Around and round she paces,
eyes on something far from this
gray North American Saturday,
this world she could've never
imagined; noises, smells,
lack of privacy, people
taking photographs of her
away.

Her back aches
for babies. She keeps
up her search
for them.

Rachael Z. Ikins

Black Bear
Angie Toh

CC0 Creative Commons, No attribution needed, Free for commercial use) https://pixabay.com/en/black-bear-black-bear-large-strong-2659033/

What is a Woman?

A few months ago I was straightening out my basement and I ran across a piece of paper. As I read it, my mind went back to 1969. I could see myself sitting in a Home Economics class designed for girls who were more academically inclined. The class was split into groups of four girls per table and everyone was listening to the teacher explain the current project. Sitting next to me was a very shy girl with a perky nose and chipmunk cheeks. Without a word, she slid a piece of paper to me. Curiously, I glanced down at it, but soon I was savoring every word.

"Did you write this?" I whispered. She nodded with a smile.

"Can I copy it? I love it." She nodded again.

When I graduated from high school, that paper was put in a box with other items from my school days that I thought were valuable. After I married, the box went into the basement of our home. For thirteen years the paper stayed in that box. Every two or three years I would browse through the box (usually when I was trying to put off cleaning the basement). However, when we moved to a new home, the box didn't move with us. My husband had cleared the basement and my box of memories went to the dump.

I was heartbroken. Memories of the box's contents flooded my mind – the letters from my classmates in second grade when I was sick for three months, the notes I had written but never given to a boy I had a crush on in fourth grade, my report cards from high school, and a few certificates of achievement.

For the next five years, the only things I had left were the yearbooks and one report card from the year I started seriously dating my now-husband (shown by a noticeable drop in my grades). All the other memories would forever-after exist only in my mind.

That was true until a few months ago when I was cleaning the basement in our next-to-new home. Because we were making half the basement into a rec room, I had to throw out as much as possible. That's when I found the piece of paper.

Thinking back, I know the paper had been in my childhood box. I'm sure of it! I had no reason to suspect the box would end up at the dump, so there was no reason for me to remove the paper. But, I'm glad I did! As I reread it now, it brings tears to my eyes.

I hope you readers enjoy this piece as much as I have. It is entitled, "Being a Woman," and the author's name is unknown. I hope the author reads this and finds out how much her essay has meant to me all these years.

It reads:

"Having a diploma may mean having an educated mind, but to be a woman you must have an educated heart.

An educated heart has learned to give and to ask nothing in return. It is kind even when kindness is not returned. It is humble before the wisdom of the more learned.

An educated heart gives encouragement, because it has felt the disappointment of failure. It applauds because it remembers the thrill of success.

An educated heart is tolerant, because it sees the faults of others as a reflection of its own. It forgives for it knows what it means to request forgiveness. It gives quiet help where others give empty promises.

An educated heart shares itself with the lonely, for it has known the heartbreak of loneliness. It sees the longing for affection that lies beneath the shyness, the love that silence conceals.

An educated heart is courageous but never rash, cautious but never cowardly. It knows no fear because it knows the power of faith.

An educated heart offers thanks for the gift of life and the chance to give the gift of love. It is grateful for the blessings that have come in place of unrealized dreams. It has searched for peace and has found it within itself.

IT IS THE HEART OF A WOMAN!"

I don't want to go back to the old days when we needed (yes, needed) songs like "These Boots Were Made for Walking" or "I am Woman … Hear Me Roar," but it saddens me to think that society has forced women to give up some of our insides simply to be considered equal to men. Can't we be equal without pretending to be identical?

Sue Vogt

Interloper
Sueann Wells

Dancing with Shadows

I love to watch my daughter dance. She has an innate sense of grace that I have yet to embody. She moves with such freedom, uninhibited by modesty and self-judgment. Gliding from one step to the next, each dance is an improvisation of lithe unencumbered limbs that know no embarrassment.

Lately, she has begun to notice herself. While prancing through the kitchen, she occasionally pauses at the sight of her reflection in the oven door. Then she leaps across the living room, bathed in golden rays, watching her shadow imitate her. She even dances with it at times, perceiving how her shadow is different yet still connected to her. Her observations have proven that it is sometimes long and lean, other times short and squat, depending on the angle of the sun.

I have always found it interesting that where there is light, there is necessarily shadow. This dichotomy exists all too clearly in motherhood as well. Despite the brightness emanating from my young children, I frequently flail in my own darkness.

Now that I am a mama, I know that I must address my shadow. I can no longer fumble through each day, seemingly unaware of the fears, frustrations, bad habits, and faulty patterns that I exhibit. Doing so would mean suffering for my children. They would fail to thrive, languishing in a pool of obscurity like the one in which I learned to swim.

And so even when I am exhausted and discouraged, I still strive to acknowledge and somehow improve on the sum of my parts: the light and the dark, the positive and the negative, the nurturing and the nagging, the artistic and the antagonistic. Sometimes it is nearly impossible to discern what originates from my shadow side because I have grown so accustomed to its omnipresence. And yet, I am committed to becoming mindful of the energy I emit. The stakes are too high to turn a blind eye.

Darkness terrified me as a child. Sometimes it still does, but I know on an intellectual level that I need not fear my shadow. Rather than run from it, I can learn from it, heal from it, teach from it. Above all, I seek to dance with my shadow self, empowered by the knowledge that there will always be light on the other side. Each day I take a step, sometimes tentatively, other times bravely, often clumsily, but always sincerely. In the meantime, I garner encouragement and inspiration from the way my daughter glows as she dances barefoot with her shadow in the late afternoon light.

Jennifer DeVille Catalano

Shadow Dancer
Jennifer DeVille Catalano

In Search of Peace

A squirrel makes an Olympics-worthy dive ten feet over to the next tree. The birds call out in their myriad voices, mixing with the chatter of rodents big and small to make an autumn cacophony in my ears this morning.

Acorns pummel the drooping teepee's roof, sounding like hail pellets.

Canadian geese honk overhead en route to the ponds that are merely a resting point as they cherish the final few weeks here.

My literary spirit awakens on this brisk, sunny autumn morning. My calves' yearning to run is squelched as I stop to record these beautiful kernels of observation. I cannot ignore the muse when she calls.

The tiniest of pebbles kicked up by human feet echo across the valley of half-naked trees. I want to stifle my cough or sniffle, not disturb the calm beauty around me. I want to stand here for hours, absorbing it into my veins. I know the 30s last night will turn to 30s during the day, and then this walk will be a bit more crisp and perhaps even … dare I suggest it … unpleasant without snow gear? I must cherish each moment I have.

I cannot control it; my small sniffle startles a squirrel and she scurries up a tree. I breathe "Scuse me" and nod to her retreating tuft. I paused too long. I must bring long johns next time. My pores ache for warmth.

Silence for a mile as I hurry through a darker valley, skip-jog up an incline, hurdle horse mounds, and come up over a crest to see the familiar neighborhood fields bathed in sunlight. I hurry onward toward that sun and its promise of warmth.

Back in civilization, people are loud. A helicopter drones overhead, a mower chugs to the south, the highway cacophony is to the north, cars zip by on the country road to the east … not exactly four directions of peace. But I feel better for my hour in the woods. I mentally make a date with myself for tomorrow. Same place. Same peace. New sights and sounds.

Serenity.

Sueann Wells

Creek Peace at Low Tide
Sueann Wells

One's Uniqueness

The rains fall with such force and strength-
as if there is an urgency
to wash away any defilement,
in order to keep the land fertile.
This can be a reminder to us;
that in order to maintain our openness
with others,
we need to continually, and vigilantly
wash away our own preconceived notions and assumptions
about people--
so that their uniqueness
can be validated and affirmed.

Ginny Riedman-Dangler

Love Grows on Trees
Jennifer DeVille Catalano

We Look into Each Other's Eyes

A crack in concrete
that I never saw
beneath the doorframe
extrudes a yawning

brown-striped garter snake.
Pencil-slim. Hungry.
Her tongue flicks
air. We bumble, hurry,

step overhead. The dogs
miss her knotted retreat,
her black-eyed glance.
She rewinds, yoyo-neat.

Our feet vibrate,
shake foyer floor.
Tails wag, smack thighs,
key clicks, door slams.

I thought they'd sniff
where her tail-tip vanished.
Breakfast obsessed them.
Whiff of snake musk banished.

Her macrame knots me
to earth, shared, identical smiles.
(Haters stalk forests)
Her tether unspools me for miles.

I whisper to no one,
our encounter, dream
this nocturnal huntress
of cooling crumble-seam.

She waits out our thunder
three floors below my bed.
Into moonlit silence once more
she pokes her head.

Rachael Z. Ikins

Infinite Charm
Jennifer DeVille Catalano

In the Woods

In the woods I find solace,
peace among trees losing leaves,
shivering in the wind,
bracing themselves for the cold winter ahead.
I kick up crunchy leaves I cannot escape.
I am an interloper with all this noise.
I don't belong.
I am disturbing the peace exponentially,
                              catastrophically.

I am the interloper,
I am the solace-seeker.
My mind races through days past, days to come.
I can hardly focus on the day at hand,
the joy I should be finding in the present.
Savor the moment.
You never know which day might be your last.
And yet I linger, I dwell,
I consider the possibilities of
past, present, and future.

I want what I cannot have.
I want the greener grass.
I want to turn back time.
And yet, I am who I am because of those choices,
all those myriad mistakes I made,
all those phenomenal choices too,
            but somehow I don't think so much about them.

I can only move forward,
put one interloping foot forward
in the peaceful woods of life.

When I feel the world caving in and
my exhaustion strangling me,
I need only step a few hundred yards
and I'm in the woods and find peace.

I want to hike every day.
I am selfish.
It brings me peace.
I can relax and unwind, decompress and
unbind the stress of the day from my heart

In the woods.

Sueann Wells

Mid-production of this anthology, "In the Woods" has been published in Just Poets' annual anthology, **Le Mot Juste** *(Foothills, 2018).*

Après Charles E. Burchfield

I just knew it
it fit a pattern
it's natural
the most logical
step stage scene
it had been
modernizing
a little each day
Impressionism passé
Cubism so yesterday
Warhol a whimpering howl
of laughter
and now a dozen –isms later
post-post-modernist nonsense
regurgitated
the -istas purged
it is safe again for me to be
a watercolor painting
of a freshwater pond
lily pads egret willow

Karla Linn Merrifield

II

Make a Change in Your World

Poets of the Resistance Resist

First they came for our words,
the most vulnerable syllables,
erasing *entitlement,*
all the better to erase entitlements.
You can't kill what doesn't exist.
If you don't mention *diversity*,
there's no need to accommodate it.

But before they could come for our books,
before their holocaust of truth fireballed
our minds, we reset our lexicon:
sutef is now *fetus*;
rednegsnart = *transgender*;
ecnedive steps in for *evidence*-based;
ecneics replaces *science*-based.

They'll never catch up.

Karla Linn Merrifield

Losing Weight

Monday I wake up aimless,
wash a window, manicure my nails.
I sip my coffee before the closet's
open maw. I start to rip clothes off hangers.
I move onto the second closet.

I yank dresser drawers open
rifle through what seems like 100
bras you bought me. Though you are
2 years' history, shame can still circle
my shoulders like shingles' burning cloak.
None of them were sexy.

I've been writing it all down this summer.
22,000 words, 75 pages; "Psycho Dykes
And Other Interruptions: Expect Delays."
Manuscript not finished.

Your athletic socks top the pile,
hard wads of political correctness.
In less time than it takes
to wash one load of laundry
I cram two loads into jumbo trash bags.
I grunt, their pendulous weight
unbalances me down the stairs.
Keys jingle from my belt loop.

I lug my bundled unmentionables into
the Goodwill.
I float back outside.
I unlock my car
I notice my friend's office building
across the parking lot, see her
head bent, tapping a keyboard.
I wrestle my phone from a back pocket.
I text her,
"I am outside.
Dieting."

Rachael Z. Ikins

Leave-taking

Dog voices carve divots
from morning's misted darkness.
One silver sleigh bell gleams
half-buried in mulch where it landed,
broken from balcony garland last winter.
Scraps of summer's purple plastic pinwheel scatter,
mixed with fall leaves.

Two morning glories sprout
from seed by the front door,
my June planting
3 floors up, fell to earth.
Insist on heaven,
dicotyledons clapping.

Around 2 a.m. tomorrow morning
a full moon/killer frost will gild them black,
etch white over all these remains that tell the story
that once,
we lived here.

Rachael Z. Ikins

Jennifer DeVille Catalano

Lost Babies

For the 800 infants' bodies discovered in a septic tank in a defunct Catholic Home for Unwed Mothers in Ireland.

Every spring a speckled starling male
dons his tux and chortles his phoebe—his robin—
his redwing—scolds from a wire above the garage
drain pipe. He convinced a mate.
I watched their courtship when I walked my dogs.
Last summer I hoped the maintenance guy wouldn't notice,
let them raise their clutch in peace.

Unexpected deluge, June morning
pale drowned body face-down
one comma in earth's memoir.
I walked past Monday, Tuesday.
Wednesday insects arrived. I buried it,
shallow mound, mulch, a few straw stems.

This spring, starlings returned to the drainpipe.
"They're smart birds," I thought, "Why?"

Yesterday morning two bodies, scraps of soul,
strewn by the trash container.
I stooped, scooped graves,
a cairn for each sibling.
One was bigger.
Neither had pin feathers.
Eyes opaque gems.
Large chick's full crop distended.

After last night's rain, a tiny skeleton rises,
floats through bark chips.
It is perfect, ribs
like fingernail clippings, ivory beak,
hollow wing-bones, sculpted eye sockets.
He has companions, now, ghost flock of three.
Maybe the groundskeeper will fill in that drainpipe.
Nothing flows out of it on wings.

Rachael Z. Ikins

Innocence
Sueann Wells

The Power of Parents

Parents, you stand at the forefront.
You are watched
You are imitated
You are adored.
You hold power; never ignore your role.
Your words are repeated.
        Animosity and hatred absorbed
Your expressions mimicked
        Disgust and contempt learned
Your opinions accepted
        Beliefs acknowledged and preserved.

What will be your legacy?
What have you instilled and left behind?
Did you model acceptance, openness, and love?
Did you teach hatred, contempt, and mistrust?
The children learned
The children repeated you
The children passed it on.
The future is our children
The future must change
Too much hatred
Too much fear
Too much contempt
The future is too negative, too divisive.

Change comes from parents
Parenting is a profession
Your most important job
      Don't blow it
      Don't teach hatred
      Don't teach fear

Be proud of your position
Model kindness, respect, courtesy
Teach your children.
They are watching.

Laila Suleiman Dahan

Beginning Again

My husband was bright-eyed and ready to start the day. My daughter woke up in a good mood, free of the lingering cough that had plagued her the week prior. Having just barely recovered from the same bug, my son and I were the last to stir. I got up despite low energy and heavy limbs. There was much to do before driving north for a family gathering that had already been postponed twice.

First came the usual yawns and good morning hugs. Then while my husband and I were trying to talk about the day's schedule, my daughter interjected in an especially dramatic voice, "I wish I had something… something to make my throat feel better."

Maybe it was my overall fatigue or the headache that accompanies a bad night's sleep, but I handled it poorly. I didn't do any active listening. I didn't squat down to eye level. I didn't acknowledge her complaint or empathize. I didn't do any decoding. Knowing that she had fallen in love with the sweet cherry flavor of cough drops the previous week, I tried to cut her off at the pass. "If your throat hurts, I can give you some ibuprofen," I told her. She stomped and huffed and crossed her arms. "You can't live on cough drops," I snapped.

That one sentence of mine was all it took to immediately change the tone in our house that morning. For weeks, my husband and I had been working on implementing new parenting techniques, and I hadn't used a single one. Feeling run-down and fed up, I spoke my mind without thinking. My husband got frustrated and I became self-conscious, aware of my mistake but in no mood to be reminded of it. He and I ignored each other and everything going on around us while getting breakfast ready.

When I finally looked up, I saw my son and my daughter sitting next to each other on the living room couch, enjoying a tea party. He wasn't pulling her hair and she wasn't screaming. There was no whining whatsoever. They were happily chatting with little china cups in their hands.

As I observed my children playing, I felt an instant softening. They weren't holding on to any bad feelings. Only the adults were still stewing, and neither of us wanted that. My husband and I slipped into the laundry room for a talk. We cleared the air and decided to begin again, this time with a change of plans. In order for everyone to have the best day possible, my son and I would stay home to get some extra rest while my husband and daughter drove to my mother-in-law's house. As the two of them were putting on their shoes and coats in the mud room, I held my son on my left hip and tucked a handful of cough drops in their travel bag with my free hand, just in case.

Jennifer DeVille Catalano

Sweet Tea
Jennifer DeVille Catalano

Dear Parents: Your children watch and learn

I remember the day when I felt I had succeeded, in some small way, as a parent. My younger son, Omar, was out playing with his friends and called to me. We lived on a lovely green quad at an American university in the United Arab Emirates. We had a nice villa, paid for by the university, and all around us were other faculty members and their families. It was a wonderful place to raise children.

I walked onto the grass to see what he needed. He was about three years old, and he looked up at me and said, "Did you see me playing with Kareem?" I was not sure who that was, so I asked him to point him out. My son lifted his little hand and pointed towards a group of little boys running and playing, and said, "There he is, the one in the red shirt!"

The cute little boy in the red shirt, Kareem, was not only in a red shirt, but he was also the only child from Nigeria in that group of boys. Kareem and his family had just arrived on campus, and they were one of the first families from an African nation in our neighborhood. What made me proud of my child that day was that when he pointed out his new friend, he did not do so based on the color of his skin, but by the color of his shirt. At that point I did feel that my parenting, though sometimes lacking, had been successful in modeling for my children an acceptance and understanding of diversity.

I was raised by a Southern Baptist from Atlanta and a Muslim from Libya. They may not have been perfect parents; after all, who has those? But I believe the one thing they did perfectly was to raise their children with no real concerns regarding the 'other.' For us, everyone was just a person. We did not get into issues of who had a better religion; no, all religions were accepted in our home. My parents had friends from every faith, and I attended weddings that ran the gamut from Muslim/Arab, Jewish/Italian, Orthodox/Greek to everything in between.

That was what it was like to be raised without any fear or mistrust or hate. I commend my parents for that part of our lives, for their openness to differences and diversity, and for never defining people by their race or religion or nationality. They modeled and taught us tolerance for all.

I learned from my parents, as do all children. I learned to be open-minded. I learned that all people are equal no matter where they come from, what they do, what god they worship, or what color their skin. People are people, we are all alike, and because of my parents I absorbed that at an early age, and was then able to transmit that acceptance to my children.

This is what we need today in order to change America, because our nation has lost its way. We are angry and divisive and want to blame everyone else for our problems. It has suddenly become okay to lash out at those who are different, who look different, were not born here, or worship in a way we are not familiar with. This is wrong. This behavior will set our country back, not make it better. We are a nation of immigrants and diversity, and we must accept and acknowledge the contributions of all.

I feel strongly that the way forward, the way to make us better, is for all parents to be cognizant of what they are teaching and transmitting to their children. Children are not born to hate; parents teach them through words and actions. All I can offer to help change this multicultural and multilingual nation is to implore parents to think twice about wanting to raise yet another generation of children taught to hate.

Laila Suleiman Dahan

New Day

*It is time to flush this turd of a year
down the commode of history.
~ Dave Berry*

The terrifying trifecta of New Year's Eve in Times
Square—
a Las Vegas-style sniper, suicide bomber, and truck attack.
Hit, blown to bits, run over. Farewell, auld lang syne.

The pervert creeps with the collective IQ
of a starfish are a breathtakingly cruel
school of priapic authority figures.

Everybody goes bonkers on cue.
The teleprompter in our frontal lobe
twists the mother tongue. We're all lying.

Fireworks over county rodeo grounds
or sparks from the hooves of Pegasus?
Does the ball drop and the year explode?

Far from New York City, here in North Fort Myers,
I resolve to have the humid desire to live another dream.

Karla Linn Merrifield

Catch More Flies With Honey

Another love song, you say,
will come on strong today.
With a number one hit
money can be made.
The feeling can be full or empty
The love can be found or lost
Try to remember the search
but forget the cost.

I believe in a treat real sweet.
I can catch more flies with honey
than with an iron pot.

A brother's love song, you say
will bring a spring bouquet.
With a number one hit
money can be made.
The passion can be past or present
The heart can be warm or broke
Try to sing about the search
and try not to croak.

I believe in a treat real sweet.
I can catch more flies with honey
than with an iron pot.

Love is the power to mend all
the tower
the strength to make a house a home
You can catch more men with honey.

I believe in a treat real sweet.
I can catch more flies with honey
than with an iron pot.

Modified from a song by Sue Vogt

Write with Light
Jennifer DeVille Catalano

Hugs are Better than Slugs

The moment he opened the door
the preacher heard the loud uproar.
As he stood spying, bottles were flying,
fists were landing, few men left standing.
He shook his head in slow-motion and thought:
They need a love lotion
They should put their arms around each other
'cause hugs are better than slugs.

One man was slumped over the bar,
his blood flowing, his breath slowing,
his eyes were adopting a raccoon disguise.
The preacher lifted the man's head and said:
You look like things aren't going very well
Why not do what I do:
Put your arms around yourself
'cause hugs are better than slugs.

The beatitude
slowly silenced
the multitude

To punch it out is easy
when someone is being sleazy.
But any nit-wit will have to admit
you're the one with true grit
because you'll catch him by surprise.

That's why I'd advise:
Just put your arms around him fast
'cause hugs are better than slugs.

Yes, put your arms around each other
'cause hugs are better than slugs.

Modified from a song by Sue Vogt

Selbstgefälligkeit erzeugt eine Katastrophe

Vor Angst erstarrt
erschrocken
hungrig nach Antworten
unbeantwortbar
Warum?
Wie konnten sie?
grell kaltblütig Völkermord
Sind Menschen gottverlassen?
verdammt?
Ohne Möglichkeiten?
Alle außer tot?

Nein.
Eine Möglichkeit
Viele Möglichkeiten.

Leben.
Leben!
Gedeihen Sie in der Welt.
Mach die Welt zu dem, was wir wollen.

Wenn wir uns selbst nicht beobachten,
wer weiß was plausibel ist.
Wir müssen für den Frieden leben,
wachsam, liebevoll, mitfühlend sein,
nicht selbstgefällig.

Wir werden leben.

Sueann Wells

This poem was written by a 17-year-old Sueann for my German V honors convocation. Though it has sat in my archives for many years now, I felt it appropriate to bring out for this anthology. I hope someone out there can read the original German. For those who cannot, fear not; the translation follows this page.

Complacency breeds disaster

Frozen with fear
scared
hungry for answers
unanswerable
Why?
How could they?
Garish, cold-blooded genocide
Are people godforsaken?
damned?
With No possibilities?
All but dead?

No.
A possibility.
Many possibilities.

Live.
Live!
Thrive in the world.
Make the world what we want it to be.

If we do not watch ourselves,
who knows what is plausible.
We must live for peace,
be vigilent, loving, compassionate,
not complacent.

We shall live.

Sueann Wells

What Peace Is

I sit under a weeping willow tree with a book in my hands. A curtain of leaves and branches droop down to the ground shielding me and the trunk from the outside world.

I climb up onto a thick branch and open my book. Nothing dares bother me up on my perch.

Birds chirp softly high in the branches using their tiny wings to keep them aloft. I feel free and calm in this peaceful spot of mine.

Kayla Wells, age 11

Afternoon Light
Jennifer DeVille Catalano

Build Bridges Not Walls

They rant; they rave.
No matter the reason
this is the season …

For change,
they say, do it their way.
Not me.
I prefer to build
Bridges of understanding
not Walls of reprimanding.
I'll build bridges not walls.

For change,
they say, do it their way.
Not me.
I prefer to build
Bridges of soft tenderness
not Walls of intolerance.
I'll build bridges not walls.

A change?
This day, I'll do it my way
I prefer to build
Bridges of communication
not Walls of isolation.
I'll build bridges not walls.

Modified from a song by Sue Vogt

Discussion Questions

1. What voices resonate with you within this volume? What inspires you to make a change in your life?

2. Inspired by what you've read, What challenges have you faced in your life? What have you done to successfully rise above them? What held you back from goals? What might you do to improve your situation? Who might you ask for help when you need it?

3. Looking around you today, What do you propose to do with the life you have? Who might need a hand? Who might you help, in a tiny way, a huge way, or somewhere in the middle? How might you help? Make a plan. Make a change.

Thank you so much for embarking on this vital mission with us.

Spread the word.

Be the best *You* you can be.

Make a Change in your own world.

About the Contributors

Jennifer DeVille Catalano is a writer, photographer, and educator whose work is regularly published in national print magazines. She lives in rural New York with her husband, two children, three cats, and a multitude of wildflowers. For more information, visit her personal website, someplaceserendipitous.com

Laila S. Dahan is an adjunct professor of writing, and edits theses for MA and PhD students in her spare time. She earned her PhD in language education, and lives in California with her two sons.

Rachael Ikins is a widely-published poet / artist from Central New York. For more information on her adventure in writing, visit www.rachaelikins.com

Karla Linn Merrifield, a National Park Artist-in-Residence, has twelve books to her credit; the newest is *Bunchberries, More Poems of Canada*. She is assistant editor and poetry book reviewer for *The Centrifugal Eye*, and a member of Just Poets (Rochester, NY), the Florida State Poetry Society, and The Author's Guild.

Ginny Riedman-Dangler works full-time in the education and mental health field in Rochester, NY. She has written poetry for many years. Her first publication, a creative non-fiction piece, was printed in the *Before They Were Our Mothers* anthology (2017).

Sue Vogt has been a poet and writer for most of her life, with publications ranging from songs in the 1980s to her foray in children's stories with her *Dinosaur Parade* (Spirited Muse Press, 2017), and memoir in her contributions to the anthologies, *Mother Muse* (2009), *Motherly Musings* (2011), and *My Mother Taught Me* (2017).

Sueann Wells is a widely-published writer, as well as freelance editor, and founder of Spirited Muse Press (spiritedmusepress.com). She is an adjunct English professor and literacy tutor, a mom of three, a Girl Scout leader, and a community volunteer doing her part to make the world a better place.